KR AUG 2014
RU Sept 5
SA FEB 2017

Copyright © 2014 by Linda Napoli. 142691-NAPO

ISBN: Softcover 978-1-4931-6590-2
      EBook   978-1-4931-6591-9

All rights reserved. No part of this book may be reproduced or transmitted in any form or by any means, electronic or mechanical, including photocopying, recording, or by any information storage and retrieval system, without permission in writing from the copyright owner.

This is a work of fiction. Names, characters, places and incidents either are the product of the author's imagination or are used fictitiously, and any resemblance to any actual persons, living or dead, events, or locales is entirely coincidental.

Rev. date: 02/20/2014

To order additional copies of this book, contact:
Xlibris LLC
1-888-795-4274
www.Xlibris.com
Orders@Xlibris.com

DEDICATION

With gratitude and respect to Mother Nature for all the gifts she gives us.